I0417106

How to Be a Good Kisser

A Complete Guide
On How to Kiss, Who to Kiss
& Where to Kiss

By

Kimberly Peters

Other Books By
Kimberly Peters

How to Get Your Ex Back!

Relationship Kick Starter!

The "Performance Plus" Series

How to Be a Good Employee!

How to Be a Good Manager!

Contents

Disclaimer

All people and situations are different. Some or all of the materials in this book may or may not be suitable for any one person or any particular situation. The writers, publishers and distributors of this book assume not responsibility for the use or application of any or all information contained in this book. The reader shall use their judgment and discretion and be totally responsible for the use or application of any and all parts of this publication. In other words, be respectful, be careful and stop anything when asked.

Introduction

When it comes to kissing, the subject can raise several different responses from people depending on the relationship and situation. A kiss can represent a symbol or expression of love, a part of a passionate response or a social acknowledgement of another person. It is amazing how the same physical process can have so many interpretations and meanings!

While the process of kissing is pretty straight forward, there are many different do's and don'ts depending on the situation and people involved. Regardless of who is involved and regardless of the situation, one thing about kissing should be that we want it to be a positive experience for both people. If, for some reason, a kiss might not be pleasurable for both people, it should not be given in the first place.

That means always treating the other person with dignity and respect. Being aware of the other person's feelings, values and morals can help in approaching kissing, and other forms of physical expression, in the proper manner. This is the cornerstone of any type of physical expression and it should be observed at all times.

In this book we are going to cover kissing in several different situations and applications. We will make suggestions and provide information and some insight but the final decision and application must always be determined by the two people involved. Their relationship, whether romantic or platonic or even just social, will be the primary driver behind the kiss.

So let's get started and see what we can do to make the kiss the perfect expression of love and friendship that it possibly can be.

Morals, Values & Feelings

Let's start off by discussing a little bit about the feelings and attitudes behind the kiss. Kissing is a personal expression of love, friendship and greeting. It can also convey passion and intimacy depending on the situation. But regardless of the situation, kissing is a physical act that should be accepted by both parties. That means that both individuals must be willing to give and receive the kiss.

Kissing must never be viewed as a hostile or aggressive act by either individual. One should never be forced to partake in any physical act without their consent. In other words, both parties must agree to what is happening.

We also need to understand that someone people might have moral or value issues and concerns which may affect the way they view and react to kissing. For example, some people might not enjoy public displays of affection. For those people, they might thoroughly enjoy kissing, and other displays of affection, in a private environment but not in public.

Other people might have religious issues or other issues that prohibit certain parts of kissing or what kissing might lead them to. For example, a woman might enjoy being kissed by a man on the first date but resist things going any further than that. In those situations, the woman's feelings should be respected.

All of this leads to one very important thing. We must always respect the other person's feelings and needs. That can only come by getting to know the person we are interested in. Kissing is a physical act and knowing the person we are kissing and understanding who they are and what they like will add a dimension to the experience.

Take things slow and always be aware of the responses and body language of your partner. If they resist or seem to pull back, then stop what you are doing and determine what you should do next. Trying to get someone to do something they have reservations about is never the right way to go.

We should approach kissing like many other aspect of a relationship. We should kiss in such a manner that both people get as much enjoyment as possible from the act. There is no need to be perfect and there is no need to try too hard or make each other uncomfortable.

The physical part of any relationship grows over time as we become more comfortable and knowledgeable with each other. An argument can be made that the emotional connection or closeness is the most fulfilling or erotic part of the kiss. In other words, sharing the experience with someone you care for is often what makes a kiss truly magic.

A great kiss is a kiss that gives both people the most of what they want at the time. Whether it is a kiss that says "I love you" or a kiss that says "I want you" we should always make certain that we are never doing something that makes the other person uncomfortable or afraid. When that happens, step back and reassure the other person that everything is OK and re-evaluate things.

Setting up the Kiss

Like many other things in life, sometimes everything is in the preparation. Those little things that we do before to help give us the very best results. When it comes to kissing, there are a few little things that can help make all the difference in the world.

In this chapter we are going to go over a few things everyone should take into consideration whether it is your first kiss or your 10,000th kiss or whether it is with someone brand new or someone you have been with for decades. Kissing never gets old and these things can help keep it fresh, positive and rewarding.

Make Sure your Lips are Soft

Soft lips are kissable lips. If they are dry or rough that can spoil even the most special or tender kiss.

Use a lip balm or gel if your lips are dried out or have rough spots on them. Don't overuse it so your lips are greasy. Just make them soft and moist.

Make Sure your Lips are Moist

Moisture helps make the lips not only kiss well, but fell good at the same time. Moist lips won't dry out and crack or split. If your lips are cracked and dry, kissing can be downright painful at times. Remember your lips are for your enjoyment and your partners as well. When they are nice and moist, kisses are better for the both of you.

Remove Heavy Amounts of Lipstick

Lipstick is nice and can make you look awesome but it can also get in the way of kissing. If you have so much lipstick on that your lips slide all over the place that is not going to help the kiss at all. Guys like to kiss lips not oil slicks. Plus, lipstick will leave marks and smudges all over when the kissing is done. While that might be a turn on later in the relationship when everything is done in private that should not be something that is done all the time.

Make Sure Breath is Clean

Kissing requires close contact and close contact with the mouth means close contact with your breath. After all, the last time we checked, the nose is right above the lips so what comes out of the lips will go straight to the nose!

That means watching what you eat and your oral hygiene as well. If you feel kissing or intimacy is going to follow that evening, stay away from the garlic or really pungent or aromatic foods. Use a mouth wash or breath mint as the situation calls for. Keeping your breath fresh will enable your partner to not only enjoy the kiss more but also hang around longer for more kisses or longer ones!

Keep Teeth and Mouth Clean

One important part of oral hygiene and fresh breath is clean teeth. Brush your teeth regularly, see your dentist and floss regularly as well. If you plan on being intimate or kissing someone later on after a meal, excuse yourself and rinse your mouth out and even floss to make sure your teeth are free from bits and pieces of food.

Very few things can turn off someone more than kissing someone and winding up with a piece of their entrée in their mouth after the kissing is done. That is not sexy, that is just gross! Keep your mouth and breath clean and fresh.

Control Saliva

Saliva is part of kissing as it is a normal response to the activities going on around the lips and the mouth. No one likes to kiss someone with a mouthful of saliva or someone who is drooling out of their mouth during the kiss.

If you have a bit of saliva in the mouth then take a short break from kisses and swallow the saliva to clear it from the mouth. Then go back to kissing after you are done. Don't swallow during the kiss if possible but even that is a better alternative than continuing to kiss with a mouthful of saliva.

Pick the Right Location

Pick a nice location for the kiss. While sometimes a kiss is a spontaneous reaction or event, most of the time it is something that is planned.

Pick a nice location that is free from distractions or other factors that might spoil or at least take something away from the kiss. The ability for both people to concentrate on the kiss and everything that goes along with it can make the experience much better and more memorable.

Beware of Public Displays of Affection

Many people have issues with public displays of affection. While some people are perfectly fine with doing just about everything in public, others might prefer doing things like kissing in private or as close to private as practical.

There might be a very real difference between kissing someone on a crowded train or bus as compared to kissing someone at their front door or in the living room. Cultural practices, upbringing, and moral values all play an important role in who and what we are. Because of this we should always respect the wishes and values of our partner. If you are the one who fells this way find a nice way to express that to your partner. This way you will not risk your partner feeling rejected if you do not respond favorably.

Kissing Basics

Sometimes the difference lies in the preparation and kissing is certainly no different. Creating the proper mood and the proper setting can mean all the difference in the world. In order for a kiss to be great, both people must want it, look forward to it, and anticipate it. But sometimes being kissed by surprise can be a wonderful experience as well. Everything lies in the preparation.

Knowing what your partner likes and dislikes comes with experience. But that doesn't mean that you cannot experiment to find out! But whether this is your first kiss or you have been kissing for years, some basics things still apply.

Though this is not an all encompassing list, this should be more than enough to get you started:

Personal Hygiene

I know we already covered this but it is part of every single kiss you give so here it is again. No kiss is going to be great if your breath smells bad, if you haven't showered in two weeks and if there are chunks of food left in your teeth from lunch. Make sure you brush and floss your teeth, shower before a date and use mouthwash if necessary. A kiss involves many senses and if one of them should be a turn off for your partner nothing else will matter.

Bring Your Partner into the Kiss

Remember that a kiss is for both people not just one. Do everything you possibly can to give the other person a pleasurable experience. Be aware of how they react. Do they want more? Do they want less? Are they an active participant or just being there for you? The more you can understand about your partner the better you will be able to make the kiss more special.

Lean In

When you kiss someone, or when someone kisses you, lean slightly towards them. This will be interpreted as a positive gesture on your part and encourage the other person to continue.

If you don't like something, or if you want to stop, gradually lean away. Try to lean away gently so you don't hurt the other person's feelings.

Close Your Eyes After You Make Contact

Once you make contact with your partner's lips, close your eyes. This will help in two ways. First, it is a more intimate gesture and second, if the other person should open their eyes, they are not staring into your wide open eyes. That might be a little scary or awkward for both of you!

Do a Few Soft and Quick Kisses to Start

Everyone likes to start a little bit slowly and gradually work into things and kissing is no different. Start with a few soft and gentle kisses and gradually work up to longer and more intimate kisses. As always, monitor the reactions of your partner to make sure they feel the same way as far as where things are going. If they resist, even a little bit, back up a bit.

Open Mouth Slightly at First.

Take it a little careful at first.

No one wants to start out getting a tongue rammed down their throat right from the start.

When you first start kissing, open your lips just slightly so more of your lips can get involved. Gradually open and pucker your lips to increase the area the kiss uses on your lips. This can be very erotic for some people.

Play off Your Partner's Moves and Responses

Kissing is something that is highly personal for both people. It is a joining or two people in an intimate form of communication. Kissing works best when both people are attuned to what each other is doing and feeling.

If your partner appears to be enjoying themselves and is a willing or even aggressive participant, then you might want to move things forward. If your partner is hesitant or reserved, you should take it slowly and bring your partner along with you gradually.

Long and Slow Kisses Can Be Very Romantic & Sexy

Speed has its time and place but a nice slow and long kiss can be very erotic and sexy.

Take your time and give your partner a nice gentle and long kiss. Explore each other and just enjoy the closeness and intimacy of the moment. Sometimes one nice long kiss is much better than 4 or 5 shorter ones! Experiment and find out what each of you likes.

Use Your Hands

Kisses involve more than just lips. Use your arms and hands to hold and caress each other. Touch each other's face, ears, back and shoulders. Depending on the state of your relationship, you might progress to other areas of the body as well. But keep in mind that once you touch certain areas of the body the focus can move from kissing to other activities. If you are not willing to go there, do not touch those areas.

If someone touches somewhere that you don't want them to touch, especially in the early stages of a relationship, just gradually take their hands and move them to another place. If someone does that to you, take the hint and do not force the issue. Be respectful of each other's needs and feelings.

Run Fingers through the Hair

One of the sexiest things you can do while kissing is run your fingers gently through your partner's hair.

You might even try gently scratching their scalp at the same time. This can add a new dimension to your kissing.

Kiss the Face and Neck

Kissing can involve more than just lips. Kissing of the face, neck and shoulders as well as the ears can heighten passion and give your kissing a new feeling. Keep in mind that this might be interpreted as an escalation so be fairly certain you and your partner are ready for this. If either party is hesitant, you aren't ready so wait.

Vary Your Technique and Approach

Variety is the spice of life and kissing is no different. Vary what you do and how you do it. Mix up gentle kisses with deeper ones. Move from the lips to the face and change your style. Don't do the same thing over and over again no matter how much your partner enjoys it. You don't want your partner to get bored and lose interest. A little excitement and suspense can be a great turn on.

Breathe Through Your Nose

No matter how much you enjoy kissing, you still have to breathe.

So kiss with your lips and breathe through your nose. If you need a few seconds to catch your breath, break the kiss and hold each other while you get your breath back. Then get right back to it!

Breathing through your move and sharing a breath can be erotic at times but you need to be careful and do this will little breathes not huge gulps of air!

Try Breathing Lightly on the Skin

Gently blowing out on the skin can be very erotic as well. Warm breath on the ears, neck or face can be a huge turn on when done at the right time. Just use a light and gentle breath and be very gentle so that your partner might not even be aware of what feels so good! A little breath goes a long way here!

Open Eyes Slowly & Smile Afterwards

When the kiss is over, gently open your eyes and smile. Look into each other's eyes and enjoy the moment. The two of you have just exchanged an intimate moment and you should enjoy it and let each other know it was a great experience.

Let Your Partner Know That Was Enjoyable.

There is nothing wrong with letting your partner know you enjoyed the kiss. You might say something like "Wow, that was great!" or something along those lines. This lets your partner know that you enjoyed what both of you just did. This will give feedback to your partner so he or she will know what to do and what not to do next time!

Use All Your Senses

Kissing and being romantic involves more than just feeling lip on lip. Kissing also involves other senses as well. You can smell your partner, experience the feeling of their breathing and what their expressions as you kiss. This allows you to experience the full effects of the kiss and not just what the lips and tongue tell you.

Process Feedback

Whenever you kiss your partner will give you clues in their responses that tell you what they like and dislike. When you are done kissing make sure to remember what those responses were.

Then, you can do even better next time. Kissing is like getting to know someone. Over time you will learn more and more about each other and you will find more things that your partner likes.

Kissing is just one part of your relationship that will grow and evolve over time. It can be a glorious and wonderful journey!

Slow Down!

Kissing can be a wonderful experience for both of you but don't rush through it. Kissing can be a very effective method of foreplay. But don't rush past the kissing jump right into the rest of the act. Give it time, enjoy each other and let things take their course.

Kissing By Itself Is Wonderful

Don't let kissing always be a precursor to other sexual activity. Sometimes it is just fine to engage in a make out session without it resulting in intercourse or other act. If you partner feels that kissing is just something you do to get to sex they might lose the enjoyment and special parts of kissing that you both should enjoy.

Communicate with Each Other!

We saved this one for last in this chapter but it is one of the most important, if not THE most important tip we can give anyone. Communicating with your partner about what you want and don't want is the very best way to ensure that both of you get the most out of the experience. Letting your partner know what you like will help them understand what to do in the future.

When telling someone what you like, use a positive type of feedback by saying something like "Wow! That was great!" But if your partner does something you didn't really care for, let them know that as well but do it in a kind and gentle way so you do not offend them in the process.

Saying something like "Next time don't push so hard" or "Next time don't put your tongue in so far" will help them understand more fully what you want and don't want. As for you, when someone tells you that they don't like something, respect that. Don't keep doing it because you like it and think that they will grow to like it. Respect their feelings and desires and talk things out if a problem might exist.

This is all designed to make kissing the most positive experience it can be for both individuals.

Because when both people enjoy it more the experience just gets better, the relationship gets stronger, and everyone is just happier and more fulfilled. And, that, my friends, is just part of what kissing is all about.

The First Kiss

The first time you kiss someone can be a very special occasion. This is when you take what can be a very awkward and even frightening step in the relationship. We may feel awkward because we are not sure how the other person will react or we might be afraid of rejection. Either way, the first kiss can be a wonderful moment in a relationship.

If there is one important thing as far as the first kiss is concerned it would be to make sure you are ready. This is likely the first semi-intimate step in a relationship and you do not want to rush it. Do not fall into the trap that society today tells you that people expect everything from a kiss to all out sex on the first date. While some people may expect and want that, most people do not go to those extremes.

Chances are you will get some indication throughout the date how your partner feels about you. If he or she takes your hand or snuggles close to you at the movies or while walking, chances are they feel comfortable and happy with you. If that's the case, then that is good for you as far as that first kiss is concerned.

But if your date is stand offish or cool to you, perhaps they do not feel the same way towards you that you feel towards them. There is nothing wrong with that as everyone is different and likes different things and different people. Just take your cues from your date and either move forward or dial things back a bit.

With all of that in mind, here are some tips and advice regarding that first kiss:

Relax

One of the toughest things about that first kiss is your nerves. If you are the man, you will likely either be nervous about whether you should attempt it or not. If you are the woman, you might be nervous about whether he will try or not. Either way, you should do your best to relax and just go with the moment. If you follow the next two items on the list your nerves should disappear for the most part.

Pick the Right Location

The first kiss should be experienced in the right setting. That means it should be in a private area or a secluded area. Now I don't mean taking your date deep in the woods, but you don't want to attempt it in a crowded restaurant or at the bus stop.

Keep in mind that this kiss is going to be one you will likely remember for a long time so try and make it special. Pick a nice area mostly free of distractions. Make it private in case your date has an issue with public displays of affection. After all, you don't know that much about the other person yet. So try and make it as easy and romantic as possible.

Set the Mood

The mood is important because you want your partner to be in a positive and happy frame of mind when you kiss them. You want them to be ready and you want them to enjoy it. It should not be hurried and it should not be pressured.

Start by setting up the mood through talking and getting to know each other better. The more of a connection you make with each other the more special the kiss will be. Wait until you are ready.

Do not allow other people to push you into anything you are not ready for. Talk to each other, tell each other you like them and if appropriate, tell the other person you had a really nice time.

Do the little things that make each other feel more comfortable and relaxed with each other. Doing this now will make that first kiss more special and memorable for both of you. It is well worth the effort.

It Doesn't have to be Perfect!

While we should do everything we can to make the first kiss special and as good as it can be, you should not expect or demand perfection. After all this is something new for both of you and there is bound to be some awkwardness. Both of you might tilt your heads in the same direction causing some awkwardness but just smile and "laugh it off". Take the pressure off and just do your best.

Kissing, like other parts of your relationship, will grow over time and become easier and more spontaneous. Don't be afraid of making a mistake or not being perfect. This is just some of the things that make the first kiss, and the beginning or any relationship, special.

Be Slow & Gentle

The first kiss should be gentle and sweet. It should show tenderness and positive feelings. It should be something that is not done out of passion but instead out of caring for the other person. Accompany the short kiss with a nice hug and then follow the lead of the other person. Maybe there will be a second kiss and maybe there won't. It will depend on the person and the situation.

Monitor the Body Language of the Other Person

Body language is a visual way to see what a person is thinking or how they are feeling. This can help you decide if the moment and the feelings are right for that first kiss. Understanding body language can help reassure you or keep you from making a mistake.

If the other person likes being close to you, that is a good sign. If they resist being close and keep their distance from you, that is a sign that they are not comfortable. If the other person makes and keeps eye contact with you as you look at them, that's a great sign. It shows they are engaged and interested. If they look away or start redirecting a conversation, that's not a good sign.

Most people are respectful of other people's feeling and will not say "NO!" outright. Instead, they will do little things like turn and let you kiss their cheek instead of their lips. This indicates the person either is not ready for the kiss or is not interested. If they respond to the kiss and take an active part, or if they give you a nice hug during or afterwards, that is a great sign.

Sometimes people say not to read very much into what people say or do. But reading and interpreting body language can make things much easier, far less nerve racking and give you a much better chance of success if you do it right.

Close Your Eyes

Closing your eyes can make the kiss much more intimate. But wait until you make contact with the lips so you can see where you are going! Closing your eyes will also help avoid an awkward moment if your partner opens their eyes and you find each other staring into each other's wide open eyes! When the kiss is done, slowly open your eyes as you break contact. This will make your partner feel special.

No Tongue!

Use your tongue for eating, drinking and talking on your date.

Do NOT use it for that first kiss. The use of the tongue signifies a much more intimate meaning to the kiss. That might be a level of intimacy the other person is not quite ready for as yet and may even be interpreted as moving too fast, too soon.

Follow your partner's lead for later kisses as far as how things should proceed. Depending on the person and the situation that might be very close at hand or quite a ways ahead. Either way, wait until things are right for introducing each other's tongues.

Not Too Long

The first kiss should be somewhat short and sweet. When it is over your partner will give you clues as to whether or not they want another kiss or a longer one. Take it slow. This is the first kiss and hopefully there will be many more in the future. Make the first one special and be patient.

Be Tender

What can I say? The first kiss should be warm and tender with just the right amount of pressure on the lips. If the situation permits, a gentle hug should accompany the kiss after it is started.

When the kiss is over and if your partner responds positively, continue the hug for a few moments to enhance the intimacy.

Make Eye Contact Afterwards

Assuming both people wanted and enjoyed the kiss; establishing eye contact afterwards is one great way to extend the intimacy level and make the experience much more special. Do not kiss and run! Stay for a moment, look into each other's eyes and say something nice if the moment calls for it.

Savor the moment and enjoy it. You only get one chance for a first kiss! Some many people, this is a special moment at the beginning of a long term romance. Relax and enjoy the moment and try not to be nervous. Just relax, do your best and you will be rewarded with a wonderful first kiss that both of you will remember!

The After Date Kiss

Sometimes when you are out on a date you might feel pressured to offer or receive a kiss as sort of an obligation for a nice night out. Or maybe you feel that you should kiss but are not sure if the other person is willing. Or maybe you just feel nervous about the whole situation. All of those responses are normal.

Fortunately there are a few things you can do to take the nervousness away and set things up for a very nice outcome for both people. Everything about kissing is being aware of the situations, the surroundings and your partner. If you can be aware of everything going on around you, you are more than half way there.

Here are a few things you can do to help make that after date or goodnight kiss the perfect way to end a special evening.

Determine the Overall Mood or Feeling.

Ask yourself how the overall date went. Did you have a good time? Were things nice and pleasant and light? Did you laugh and have fun/ did you find each other interesting? Did you find you both have things in common?

If you answered most of those questions with a "YES!" then you have a pretty good idea that the experience was good for the other person and you know that you both probably feel the same way. So you might consider trying for a good night kiss as a way to end the evening on a high and more pleasant note. After all, everything else went well and you both enjoyed each other so if you are game, you can at least try!

But if you answered any or all of the questions with a "No!" or "Heck No!" then perhaps you should consider a hearty hand shake and a rapid sprint to the car or taxi. There is no sense prolonging what has been a long night or date any further.

Kissing should be something positive and not something done because you feel you have to and they feel they need to accept. If you had a horrible time and offered a kiss good night, you might send the wrong message to the other person. After all, you might have had a poor time and they might have enjoyed it. You never know.

Establish Physical Contact First

Sometimes you are unsure whether or not the other person is ready for a kiss. Perhaps it is the first date or you are not sure how the other person feels. If this is the case, try and establish other physical contact first.

Place your hand on the shoulder while you are walking or take your partners hand. If you want to go further, try putting your arm in hers or walking with your arm around his or her waist. If your partner responds positively that is an indication that he or she might be ready for the kiss. If they pull away or resist the gesture, you probably need to give them more time.

Monitor Body Language

Body language will tell you a lot about how someone feels. If they get closer that indicates a positive response and that they feel safe and secure with you. If they pull away or keep their distance, you still have to establish that safe and secure feeling. Naturally if they smile and laugh, that is good. If they frown and sob uncontrollably, that is not so good.

But simple gestures can speak volumes about a person's state of mind.

If your partner appears relaxed and comfortable, that indicates they have positive feelings about the date and about you. If they are nervous or appeared bored or keep looking at their watch, that means they wish the evening was over and you had already left.

Maintain Eye Contact Before

A kiss is a physical gesture of familiarity or intimacy depending on the situation. Because of this, it makes sense that you should establish a certain degree of intimacy before the kiss. That means looking into the person's eyes and establishing eye contact before the kiss begins.

You might also start with a nice hug and pull back slightly, look into each other's eyes, and if the response calls for it, then have a nice good night kiss. Do not rush it. Take your time. Remember this is not only for your enjoyment but for your partner's enjoyment as well!

Keep it Simple.

The after date kiss should be simple, gentle and slow. It should be intended as a nice way to end the night and not as a prelude of what you hope will soon follow.

There should be no pressure, both people should be willing and the experience should be positive for both people.

Do not think too much about what it means. Just do it when the situation calls for it and see where it takes you. Think of it as the first step of many you will hope will follow.

No Tongue!

Unless you are advanced in your relationship, keep your tongue inside your mouth during the after date kiss. You can pucker slightly and even open your mouth but keep the tongue inside until you are really sure it should become part of the process.

The after date kiss on the first date should be tongue free most of the time unless something else is really going on between the two of you. Keep it simple, keep it conservative and keep it gentle and loving. That is what the after date kiss should always be. A perfect end to a perfect date.

Follow Your Partner's Lead during and After the Kiss

One question that often comes up is "What is the right way to proceed?"

There is no perfect response to that question. As we have said everyone is different and everyone has their own thoughts and expectations. The only way to make certain is to follow the lead of your partner and see the way he or she reacts in your presence. Even then there is a certain amount of guesswork.

Sometimes the first kiss leads to a second, then a third and then from there who knows? But sometimes the first kiss is the last kiss of the evening and it should end on a positive note. Look at your partner, understand how he or she feels and respond appropriately.

It is NOT an Obligation!

Some people feel that an after date kiss is an obligation. Guys might feel that because they paid for the date they deserve a good night kiss. Women might feel that they owe the guy a kiss because he took them out. For the record, both those views are dead wrong. Any kind of contact, be it kissing or anything else, should be done because both people WANT it to happen not because they feel it is supposed to happen.

Kissing and intimacy is not some kind of currency that is used to compensate people for their time or their money.

Instead, intimacy and kissing should be used to express feelings and emotions that both people want to express at that time and in that place. If any of these conditions are not met, then nothing should take place. If it does, it might send the wrong message to one or both people.

Advanced Kissing

As relationships go forward and become more intimate, people tend to get more comfortable and more trusting. They usually become more confident and willing to try new or different things. They become more adventurous and may even allow certain feelings and values to be altered to accommodate the other person within the relationship.

When this happens it is important not to abuse or destroy the trust that has been built. Perhaps the best advice for most people is to take things slow and gradually introduce new or more intense activities and techniques. Your aim should be to bring each other along slowly and not overwhelm anyone with a sudden expression that is too ambitious or intimidating.

So please keep that in mind when you consider introducing any of the following into your relationship. It is all right to suggest something new to your partner. But if they refuse, respect their decision. If they seem apprehensive then take it slow and gradual. If at any time in the process your partner tells you to stop, stop. Do not continue and NEVER force your partner to do something you do not wish to do.

When it comes to requests your partner might make of you, consider the request and how you feel about it. It is all right to do something because you want to bring pleasure to your partner. That is a reflection of your love and caring for that person. But if something is really a turn off or off limits, explain why you are not willing to do what they ask. While an explanation is not mandatory, explaining why you won't do something is likely going to be easier on your partner than an outright refusal.

As you read through these ideas, keep in mind that sometimes less is more. Being gentle is often more sexy and erotic and will have a better response than doing something too hard. Start out slow and gentle and then follow your partner's lead about whether they want it harder or faster or softer or slower. Everyone has their own preferences when it comes to kissing and other activities.

Kiss Other Parts of the Body

Kissing does not have to be limited to the lips. Most people like to have their face and ears and shoulders kissed as well. There are other erogenous zones as well. The nipples inner thighs and other areas are especially sensitive. If you relationship has reached that stage, and your partner is willing, experiment and see what your partner really likes. If they like it, continue. If they don't just stop.

Kiss & Suck on the Earlobe

The ears can be a very sensitive and pleasurable part of the body to kiss and suck without becoming too bold. The key is to be gentle and slow. Suck lightly and even try gently blowing on the ear as well. Gently nibble and kiss all around the ear including the back of the ear and where the ear meets the neck.

Kiss the Face

Don't neglect the rest of the face when kissing. Kiss the cheeks and forehead and even the nose. Cup both cheeks and slowly kiss around the face. That can be extremely erotic and pleasurable.

Caress the Roof of the Mouth

If your partner is willing, use your tongue to caress and trace the upper part of the mouth. That can be very sensitive and enjoyable. But beware that it does require a good deal of the tongue being in the mouth and some people might find that not all that appealing. This is one of those things you might have to ease into or talk about first so your partner knows what you are trying to do.

Nibble & Bite (Gently)

Gentle is the rule here. Some parts of the body will respond favorably to a GENTLE nibble or two. The ears, lips nipples and other areas are the prime targets for a quick nibble. Keep in mind that there often is a very fine line between pleasure and outright pain! Keep it slow and gentle at all times unless instructed otherwise.

Suck the Lips & Tongue

If your partner is willing, try sucking on the tongue when it is inserted into your mouth. Suck gently on the lips as well. This can be very erotic if your partner enjoys this type of contact. Don't do it for long periods of time or over and over.

Introduce it every once in a while as a way of changing your technique and keeping your partner guessing!

Whisper in the Ear

As we said before, kissing involves more than just the feeling in your lips. Kissing involves all the senses and hearing is definitely one of them. Whisper nice things into your partner's ears as you touch each other. Whisper encouragement, suggestions and other comments to let your partner know what you want them to do. If you really want to ratchet things up a bit, ask them what you can do for them! (But be prepared for the answer!)

Kiss Navel, Feet & Hands

The navel can be a sensitive and stimulating area to kiss. The feet and hands are also erotic areas. Combining a kiss with a slow and nice massage can work wonders and help remove tension and stress at the same time! Which brings us to:

A Nice Massage Goes Well!

Kissing is a great way to show your partner how much you care.

Adding a slow and romantic massage to the mix can bring the passion and reactions to a whole other level. Massages are helpful in letting people relax and just surrender themselves to their partner. It requires a certain amount of trust and security but it can add a new dimension to your kissing and other activities.

One word of caution. When you massage someone, where you massage can have an entirely different meaning. Once you go to those places your massage can go in an entirely new direction and you should be reasonably certain that your partner wants to go in that direction. A nice relaxing massage can turn into a sexual foreplay if sex organs are massaged or kissed or sucked. While that is not a bad thing some of the time, you do not want a nice massage to turn into something frustrating for either of you.

Kiss in the Dark

Turning out the lights and fooling around in the dark adds a certain amount of mystery to your kisses. Because you really can't see where the lips and hands are going to go next, there will be more anticipation added to the process and this can be a real turn on. If both of you like it, then go for it.

This can also be helpful if your partner is shy or self conscious for any reason.

Turning the lights out might result in fewer inhibitions and more freedom and relaxation. Since that is what we are all looking for, turning out the lights may turn on both of you!

There are many ways to please and excite your partner and no one should limit themselves to what is written in a book or a magazine. Use these tips as a starting point and take it from there. If you think you and your partner might enjoy something, bring it up to your partner. If it sounds nice then give it a try. If one or both of you are against it, table the thought at least for now. As things progress what was off limits yesterday might be more interesting tomorrow.

But it bears repeating one more time. Something should be agreeable to both partners before it is a part of your kissing or sex life. If one person is against it, both partners should agree not to do that. If one partner still insists and forces the other to do something they do not want to do or are not ready for, that should considered a relationship breaker.

No one should have to put up with any kind of physical or emotional abuse as part of their physical relationship. Each partner should have enough respect and caring for the other to never subject that partner to any kind of abusive behavior. If they do, it is time to show that partner to the door.

Social or Non Romantic Kissing

Social kissing is generally thought of as an acknowledgement or greeting of a non romantic friend or relative. This is where you meet someone and say hello and offer them a kiss on the cheek or other similar type greeting. There is no romantic or sexual component to the relationship.

In some cultures kissing is a routine and normal type of greeting even between members of the same sex. That means in some cultures men will kiss each other instead of shaking hands. While this might be viewed as strange and make some people uncomfortable, it should be known that this is a cultural issue and nothing more.

So here are some things you should be aware of when it comes to social kissing:

Be Aware of Social Culture

As we just stated, some cultures consider kissing an acceptable greeting for people of all sexes. So when interacting with people of that culture, they might attempt to kiss you because they consider that normal and appropriate.

Unless it makes you feel uncomfortable or uneasy, it usually is best to recognize the culture aspect and graciously accept the kiss. Nothing intimate or forward is meant by the gesture. It is strictly a cultural issue and nothing more. If the person tries to make it something more then you should resist if that is not what you want.

Reserved for People You Care For

Outside of the cultural aspect, kissing as a form of greeting or acknowledgment is something that should be reserved for people you care for. For other people, a handshake is more appropriate.

For example, your close friends would get kisses while the newspaper delivery person would get a handshake and nothing more. You should choose the type of greeting you want for each person. If it feels comfortable and the setting and situations is appropriate, go ahead and greet that person with a kiss.

Otherwise, play it safe and go with the handshake!

Remove Most of Your Lipstick

If this is a social greeting, go light on the lipstick. The last thing someone will want it to go through the day or evening with lipstick stains on their face or clothes. This might be a consideration when you are applying makeup prior to meeting people.

Kiss once or Twice on the Cheek.

The social kiss is supposed to have no romantic or sexual component to it. Because of this, one or two short kisses to the cheek, not the lips, is appropriate. If it is a close member of the opposite sex, then perhaps the lips would be OK, but for the vast majority of situations, stick with the cheek. You can always be directed to the lips afterwards!

Kissing on the Forehead are Considered More Romantic

Stay away from kissing on the forehead for social greetings. That, for some unknown reason, is seen as more romantic kissing than social kissing.

One exception to that might be greeting a small child where a kiss to the forehead would still be considered very innocent.

Keep it Short & Sweet. Do Not Send Wrong Message

Sometimes the lines between social and romantic might get a bit blurred. Maybe you have met someone you used to have a romantic relationship with but now it is strictly platonic. In those cases be very sure you do not send the wrong message with your kiss!

The kiss should signify that you acknowledge their presence. Not that you want to re=establish the relationship and take up where you left off. Do not be overly aggressive in your kiss and keep it short and sweet and nothing more. The last thing you want to do is make someone believe you want more out of the situation than you really do!

Make Your Intentions Clear. Offer Cheek.

To take all guesswork out of a social kiss, offer the cheek. Even if someone is aiming for the lips, if you don't want that, turn your head at the last minute and let them kiss your cheek. Then, smile, be gracious and move on.

That will leave no doubt what you wanted and what you intended. If the other person still doesn't get the memo, make your intentions very clear!

Follow the Lead of the Other Person

Some people, regardless of culture, are not comfortable with kissing of any kind from friends and associates. If you are like that, or if someone you know is like that, there is nothing negative or wrong about gently rebuffing the gesture and offering your hand instead.

For example some people have a fear of germs and do not like the idea of a stranger or casual acquaintance lips touching their lips or cheek. Some might not even like shaking hands but that is much rarer. Offer your hand or tell someone you are coming down with something or don't feel well. Be gracious and give the other person an "out" with grace.

The Intimate Kiss

Caution: This chapter contains some explicit topics and sexual references. If this information is objectionable to you we suggest you skip this chapter entirely.

As your relationship progresses, kissing will often be used a foreplay to get both you and your partner into the mood for sex. This is perfectly fine if that is what both people want. Kissing can be a highly erotic activity that can really get your heart rate going and your passions flaming.

Here are a few things you can do to use kissing to create the best sexual experience for both people:

Sexually Transmitted Diseases (STD)

Always remember that contact with any part of the body, especially intimate areas, can result in sharing of germs, diseases and infections.

Be sure to know if your partner has any diseases or infections.

But do not take their response for granted. Both partners should assume responsibility and take adequate precautions to protect their health. Condoms are a good start but even they DO NOT provide adequate protection against all STD's.

Though this can be an awkward topic to bring up early in the relationship, it is something that is important and it should be a concern to everyone. Ask your partner and when your partner asks you, be 100% honest in your response. If there are any issues, consult with your doctor about precautions and which activities might be of higher risk for your situation.

Cup the Face in Your Hands

Take your partners face in your hands and cup it as you kiss them. Run your hands through their hair and around their neck. I light scratching of the scalp can give your partner the chills!

The "A-Frame" Stance

Stand together with your legs spread slightly apart and press your hips towards each other.

This will quickly raise the heat on your kisses. Pressing the hips together will help form an intimate connection between you and your partner!

Explore Sensitive Areas with Your Hands

As you kiss, roam your hands around the back and other areas of your partner's body. Do not head straight for the "good places" but instead, work up to that. After a little while caress the breasts lightly as you kiss. This might be greeted with a moan or other positive reaction.

For the woman, you might want to massage the inside of his thighs gently and then move up to his groin. Gentle is the key especially in the beginning. You both can be a little less gentle as things heat up.

A Tongue in the Ear

Take a break from kissing and LIGHTLY insert the tip into the ear. Do it gently and quickly to give your partner a little bit of excitement. Some people like this but some don't. Try it and see how your partner reacts!

The Breasts

Kissing and sucking on the breasts is something both men and woman enjoy. The nipple is a very sensitive area and gently sucking and kissing it will help really get your partner in the mood. This works for both men and women.

Kissing the Thighs

Running your fingertips up each thigh lightly can send shivers through your partner. Start above the knee and slowly run your fingers up to just before the crotch. Do not go any further the first two or three times to build up expectations. Then start and go all the way up. You will most likely hear a moan or two of pleasure.

A variation of this would be to start kissing the inner thighs always stopping just short of where your partner really wants you to go. Then, when you feel the time is right, go further!

Kissing Intimate Areas

While oral sex and kissing of the penis and vagina can be a wonderful experience for both partners, this is something many people do not feel comfortable with.

This can be because they feel those areas are not areas one should place their lips of tongue or because they just don't enjoy that type of activity.

But if you and your partner are comfortable with this then by all means, go ahead. But be careful and be gentle. These areas are very sensitive and every little nibble or sucking can result in powerful sensations. If you get too aggressive or forceful, what once felt good can quickly become painful.

Your partner may also feel uneasy about kissing you or your lips after they have been "down there". This is something you need to work out with your partner. Maybe you could have a warm washcloth or tissue to wipe your face after you are done. Whatever works between you and your partner is what you should do.

Another possibility is to do this kind of activity in the shower where you can direct your face towards the water when you are through. This will allow you to wash away any bodily fluids which are on your lips freeing you both to continue with what you are doing.

Kiss During Sex

A lot of men and women get so caught up in the sex act itself they stop kissing completely.

They concentrate on other things and other feelings and the kiss becomes secondary until after orgasm. The truth is that kissing during sex is one of the greatest pleasures and will heighten the overall enjoyment and result in a better and more powerful orgasm.

While some positions might make kissing difficult or even impossible, there are positions that will enable both partners to kiss each other easily. Make it a priority to switch to one of these positions from time to time to reestablish the kiss as part of your lovemaking. You will both thank each other when you are finished. Another useful tip: Kissing each other during orgasm can be a powerful experience for both of you! Try it!

Communicate, Communicate

When kisses during sex, gently lead your partner in the direction you want them to go. Push harder if you want your partner to be more forceful. Gently move away or push him away if you want them to be gentler. Give them feedback on what they are doing and let them know what you want.

Feedback needn't be verbal. A moan or gasp is all that is needed for your partner to know you like something. Don't be afraid to let your partner know something feels good. Be engaged and be noisy if that is what you feel like doing.

It is important the both of you build a strong emotional connection and feel safe and secure with one another. Sex is something that is constantly changing with new things being introduced from time to time. Whenever something new is introduced there is going to be apprehension on someone's part. When there is a strong feeling of safety and security both partners know the other would never do anything to hurt them or cause them pain. These feelings are critical to your sec life and should be treasured and protected at all costs.

Kissing Tips

Now that we have mastered the basics, and perhaps a few advanced techniques as well, it is time to maybe go over a few things and give you a few ideas to help you spice things up and make things different. Keep in mind that it is always about what is good for BOTH people and not just one or the other.

If you and your partner like and enjoy something, that's perfectly fine as long as there is no health risk or harm involved. If one of you does not like something, it is best to try something else so both people are engaged and happy with the relationship.

Always Make Eye Contact

Making eye contact increases the emotional aspect of the kiss. It makes it deeper and more meaningful to both people. It helps break down barriers and increases the level of security between the two people.

A lot of the time this attachment and emotional fulfillment will take the kiss to another level.

Make Your Mouth Taste Sweet

Why not consider changing the taste of your mouth so your partner will experience a different taste every now or then? Eat a piece of fruit such as a strawberry and then kiss deeply savoring the flavor. This can be a huge turn-on for a lot of people.

You can even drip juice or chocolate sauce or your favorite liquor on your partner's body and kiss and lick it off. This could send you and your partner through the roof with excitement and pleasure.

Use your Full Lips

When you kiss, use the full area of your lips from time to time. Pucker up and use the entire lip to make the kiss more intimate and exciting. Don't just use the very tip of the lip unless this is a social kiss. If it is a romantic or intimate kiss, use the full surface area of the lip. Kiss the top of the lip, the sides and the bottom. Move around and vary the pressure as well.

Make Your Lips Warm

Another way you can change things is to vary the temperature of the mouth. Kiss after drinking a hot beverage (but make sure the taste is not a turn-off!). Drinking a bit of hot or warm water will help make the kiss different.

Cold can also have the same effect especially when kissing sensitive areas of the body. Slip an ice cube into your mouth and surprise your partner with a cool sensation! Do not make it too cold as this might cause pain or discomfort. Experiment a little to find out what your partner likes and dislikes and then take it from there.

Head to Toe

There are a lot of sensitive spots on the human body. Search for them, find them and use them! What more can I say. A little exploration (within acceptable bounds for your partner) can make things extremely erotic and exciting.

Look into Each Other's Eyes

While kissing is nice and stimulating, you should come up for air every once in a while.

Just look into each other's eyes, hug or hold each other and just savor the closeness and togetherness. After all, that is part of any physical relationship.

You might whisper a few things to your partner or just look into their eyes and run your fingers through their hair. Giving yourself a break helps you and your lips rest a little bit before you start things up again.

Compliment Your Partner

Everyone loves to hear nice things about themselves and your partner is no different. Let them know how pretty or special they are. Tell them how much they mean to you. Say nice things to make your partner feel needed and special. This will help increase the bond between the two of you and make the relationship stronger.

However, always consider the stage of your relationship before you say something. You do not want to say something that might scare or intimidate your partner. For example, on your first date you should not tell someone they mean the world to you and that you want to have 5 kids and a condo in the hills!

The reaction to that would be fear and the thought that you were not being sincere in what you say.

Remember that there are people out there who will say and do anything in order to get what they want from someone. Always be sincere, honest and respectful whenever you say anything to your partner.

Control the Amount of Saliva

When you take a break, use that opportunity to swallow excess saliva. Any time the mouth is stimulated it will produce saliva. No one likes kissing someone with a mouthful of saliva. Do monitor the amount of saliva and take a short break to swallow. It is usually awkward to swallow in the middle of a kiss.

After Sex Kissing

When kissing leads to sexual relations, it is important to also use kissing as a way to end the sexual act and calm each other down. Do not finish and hop out of bed and get dressed so you can watch the game. Lay there and hold each other and kiss each other. Give yourself and your partner time to enjoy the moment and enjoy being with you. Who knows, if you do this long enough you just might be ready for round two!

Don't Always Make Kissing a Prelude to Sex

I guess this is for the guys out there but it can apply to both sexes.

Don't always make kissing something that leads to intercourse or any other sex act. Kissing is great foreplay but it should also be a way of expressing one's feelings and attraction for someone else without the need to shed clothes and go at it.

This is where communication comes into play. Both partners must be open and honest with each other throughout their relationship. They need to know what they do that it might cause the other person to desire sexual or what things might turn the moment from a kissing situation into a sexual one.

For example, if you are kissing and your hands should roam to her breast that can change the moment quickly for the woman. The same applies to caressing the penis of the man during kissing. When either partner does that they are saying to the other "I want sex now". While this is often the idea of both partners, there will be times when one of you just wants to be held and kissed without it going further.

Sometimes one person has something different in mind that the other when it comes to what is going to happen next.

In those cases, try to be understanding and talk about the situation so the other person does not feel rejected and hurt. This can be difficult but through communication and understanding you will get to know more about your partner and what they want, feel and need.

Kissing Mistakes

As with most things in life, there are some things that you should do and some things you should never do. In this chapter we are going to discuss some of the most common mistakes when it comes to kissing. Most of these are completely avoidable if you just do a few easy things.

Here are just a few common mistakes you should be aware of as it pertains to kissing your partner:

Too Much, Too Soon

Sometimes emotions and desires get away from us and hormones override common sense and feelings. When this happens short and gentle kissing can go to intense and lingering kisses in a matter of seconds. Most people are caught off guard by such a rapid escalation and this is rarely a good thing.

A good rule of thumb would be the less time you two have been together the slower and more reserved your escalations should be. Take your time with a new partner and proceed slowly and at a pace that you and your partner seem to find appropriate. Going too fast can destroy the trust and security that is so important in any relationship.

Too Hard

No one wants to have their lips smashed so hard their teeth almost come through to the outside. Though passions will sometimes take over and make kisses slightly harder than they should be or that you want them to be, always be aware that pain is not part of normal kissing.

If you have a choice or going too hard or being too soft, opt for being too soft. Your partner can gently lead you into being more forceful and aggressive by their actions and this would be a turn on for both of you. But going to hard and being pulled away from may be a response that would be taken very negatively. No matter what, open the lines of communication afterwards and let your partner know how you feel.

Too Aggressive

Kissing can often lead to other things and when this happens you should proceed in a controlled manner, especially at first until you are familiar with your partner. Try to move ahead at a speed that is mutually agreeable and satisfying to your partner.

Keep in mind that many people have fears or inhibitions that they have to deal with. They might want you to do something but are afraid to let you. If this is the case you should talk this out and make each other aware of their feelings and fears. Then you can proceed slowly and with caution and see how things go.

Too Messy

Unless you are really into the throws of passion, keep the slobbering to a minimum. Most people do not like to experience a ton of saliva in their mouths or all over their bodies. Keep the lips moist but clean and not dripping with saliva. Discreetly wipe your lips to keep them from getting too wet.

Poor Hygiene

Body odor, dirty skin, gross looking teeth, bad breath and other things are usually a huge turn-off.

Do not expect your partner to give you a big hug and a deep kiss if you haven't showered since a week ago last Thursday!

Plan ahead if you expect to be kissing someone. Take a shower, brush and floss your teeth, use a mouthwash if needed and just care of your overall personal hygiene. Doing this also shows a certain level of respect for your partner as well as respect for yourself.

Wrong Location

While there are a lot of places on the body you can kiss, some might be off limits for your partner for several reasons. You need to respect the boundaries you partners places on the relationship.

If your partner is not ready or willing, don't do it. Follow their lead for when they might be ready. NEVER force yourself on your partner. To do that can destroy the bonds of trust and respect the two of you have built with each other.

Too Intense

Sometimes kissing can get really passionate. When this happens kisses can get too hard, become too fast and emotions and physical responses get too high and overwhelming.

it can be difficult to remain in control of yourself in these situations, keep in mind that you can do harm to your partner and your relationship if you let things get too far out of hand.

For example, your partner might like a little nibble every now and then but that nibble could turn into a painful bite when you are consumed with passion. Establish boundaries and stay within them until your partner leads you in another direction.

Intense physical activity of any kind can be intimidating and downright scary for some people. Always keep this in mind and watch what you do and how you do it. If you should go too far, pull back and apologize. Comfort your partner so they retain the secure feeling they have with you. If you make your partner afraid or concerned about what might happen next, that will spoil any kind of activity that the two of you might engage in.

Conclusion

When it comes to kissing, it is often best to just be ware of certain things but to let your instincts and caring for the other individual take over and play a major role. If you truly care about the other person, and allow those feelings to show through in your kissing, most everything else will fall in line.

After all, we want kissing to be a positive and enjoyable activity for both people. Not just one or the other but both. That way both people will be responsive and look forward to the experience and not come to avoid or resist it.

The best thing you can do is follow the guidelines in this book and combine them with your common sense. If a little voice tells you not to do something, it might be best to listen to that voice. If something in your head tells you it might not be smart to try something at that moment that is probably a good idea as well. Those "little voices" often contain a lot of truth and wisdom.

Another great approach, especially at the start of the relationship, is to ask yourself what you think the other person would really enjoy. Not what you would enjoy, but what they would enjoy. If you make the other person the focus of your efforts and actions, you will almost always experience a greater chance of success than if you just do what you want to do.

Remember that a relationship of any kind always does better and grows faster when there is great communication between both people. Do not be afraid to talk to your partner and tell them what you like and what you dislike. Each is equally important. If your partner does something that you don't like that can be a mood changer and if you don't let them know it may continue to happen. Be gentle, be kind and let them know what you want.

Last, but most certainly not least, remember that kissing is a form of expression and affection. It involves physical and emotional needs and feeling. It involves cultural aspects and differences as well as values and morals. You cannot separate the act of kissing from any or all of those factors. Being to understand each of them and take them into consideration will allow you to initiate and respond in a much more appropriate and positive manner.

So go ahead, brush those teeth, put on a big smile and pucker up!